PUFFIN BOOKS

A PICNIC OF POE~~TRY~~

Poems about food

Why is it
So lit~~tle~~ ~~to~~ smell?
These ~~odou~~rs I love well:

The smel~~l o~~f coffee, freshly ground;
Of rich plum pudding, holly-crowned;
Or onions fried, and deeply browned.

A feast of words all about the growing, buying, selling, cooking and eating or *not* eating of food. With poems from all around the world by poets as diverse as Seamus Heaney, John Agard, Eleanor Farjeon, Ogden Nash, Maya Angelou and A. A. Milne, this collection is certain to become a favourite with everyone.

Anne Harvey trained at the Guildhall School of Music and Drama and now combines her work as an actress and director with her work in the world of poetry. She is a freelance writer, lecturer and broadcaster, an examiner in speech and drama, and regularly adjudicates at poetry and drama festivals. She is an active member of the Poetry Society. Anne Harvey lives and works in London.

A PICNIC OF POETRY

Poems about food and drink

Selected by Anne Harvey
Illustrated by Helen Read

PUFFIN BOOKS

PUFFIN BOOKS

Published by the Penguin Group
27 Wrights Lane, London W8 5TZ, England
Viking Penguin Inc., 40 West 23rd Street, New York, New York 10010, USA
Penguin Books Australia Ltd, Ringwood, Victoria, Australia
Penguin Books Canada Ltd, 2801 John Street, Markham, Ontario, Canada L3R 1B4
Penguin Books (NZ) Ltd, 182–190 Wairau Road, Auckland 10, New Zealand

Penguin Books Ltd, Registered Offices: Harmondsworth, Middlesex, England

First published by Blackie and Son Ltd 1988
Published in Puffin Books 1990
1 3 5 7 9 10 8 6 4 2

Made and printed in Great Britain by
Richard Clay Ltd, Bungay, Suffolk

CONTENTS

Growing   9

Shopping   41

Cooking   57

Eating and Drinking 79

Snacks   131

For my son, Matthew, who is a
great lover of good food, in poetry
and especially on the plate.

These I have loved: White plates and cups, clean-
gleaming,
Ringed with blue lines . . . the strong crust
Of friendly bread; and many tasting food . . .

Rupert Brooke

INTRODUCTION

When I visit schools and libraries to give readings from my
poetry anthologies teachers and children often ask: 'What made
you choose that particular idea—War, or Animals or People?' I
expect I'll be asked about this book: 'Why Food?', so I've been
giving that some thought.

Everybody enjoys food. We may have different tastes—some
of us will go 'Ugh! Disgusting!' and make a face, while others go
'Aaah! Delicious!' and look dreamy when faced with the same
plateful, but none of us really believes the poem on page 128 that
says 'It would be jolly if we didn't have to eat.' We know it
would be boring and miserable. Mealtimes break up the day
wonderfully, and are something to look forward to especially on
those dull days when nothing exciting is happening. While we're
struggling with a problem at school, or doing jobs at home or
work, our imaginations drift towards food. 'What's for lunch, or
tea, or supper?'

It certainly seems that many poets write about food and drink,
in fact are a hungry, thirsty lot. Looking back in my own life,
certainly food and meals stand out in my memories. I can recall
being offered a ripe, juicy pear by a kind lady on a bus one day,
just after I'd been travel sick. And I remember a camping picnic
where we had cornflakes, with condensed milk and lemon jelly all
mixed together. And there was a beautiful cake made in the shape

7

of a duck pond with model ducks and trees for my ninth birthday, spent in hospital. Best of all was the indescribable joy of a banana after the Second World War when they had been so long rationed.

As a child I disliked greens (even the very dark green cabbage that my grandmother called 'blues' thinking this might tempt me) so I can sympathise with David King on page 100. I also disliked peanut butter, fat on meat and grapefruit. Nowadays I don't eat any meat at all, but simply adore grapefruit and peanut butter. Tastes can change. The same thing can happen with poetry. You may enjoy some of these poems at once and swallow them whole or gobble them up quickly. Others may need chewing over slowly, savouring for a while. You may not be able to digest them or to enjoy their flavour immediately. But, as with food, you may grow to like them on a second or third try.

Subtle tastes in cooking take time to grow on us. Poems with unusual ideas (perhaps written in the style of another century) and poems with unfamiliar words (that need the help of a dictionary) are worth a second chance. Suddenly you'll find everything falls into place. You'll see what the poet means. A picture will form in your mind's eye.

I've tried to include poems about all kinds of food, but there are gaps. No editor ever really feels completely satisfied with the final choice. I myself always feel as I hand in my final proofs: 'Help! Are there wonderful poems hiding from me in corners of libraries or other people's bookshelves?'

I was pleased to find poems on some of the delicious fruits we can now buy more easily in the supermarkets—like lychees, persimmons, pomegranates and mangoes, as well as poems from other countries.

Perhaps you'll read this introduction as an hors d'oeuvre, or starter, to a large meal—a feast of words all about the growing, buying, selling, cooking, eating (not forgetting the snacks) of food.

Anne Harvey

Growing

Digging

Today I think
Only with scents,—scents dead leaves yield,
And bracken, and wild carrot's seed,
And the square mustard field;

Odours that rise
When the spade wounds the root of tree,
Rose, currant, raspberry, or goutweed,
Rhubarb or celery;

The smoke's smell, too,
Flowing from where a bonfire burns
The dead, the waste, the dangerous,
And all to sweetness turns.

It is enough
To smell, to crumble the dark earth,
While the robin sings over again
Sad songs of Autumn mirth.

Edward Thomas

Rice-Planting

From early morning the cultivator
is roaring
Uncle in a rubber coat walks back and forth.
Brother throws bundles of young rice plants
From the road into the flooded paddy-field.
One bundle after another
Flies like a ball, making a loud splash.
While I stand watching,
Lines of green plants are formed.
Frogs are singing loudly.

Tokiyo Yamada

My Garden

I've a garden of my own
    Which one day you must come to see.
You'd be surprised, the things I've grown.
    They make a rare variety.
Besides the flowers there's useful things,
Like scarlet runners climbing strings.

Ther's two potatoes by the beans,
    And half a row of radishes,
Five onions, several curly greens,
    And three tremendous cabbages.
They'd be as fine as you could see
If only snails would let them be.

Tomatoes, too, I try to grow
　　In one snug corner by the wall.
They never get much sun, and so
　　As yet they're rather hard and small.
But they'll have time to ripen still,
Spread on a sunny windowsill.

I put some work in every day
　　One day off means I get behind.
I dig, and keep the weeds away
　　And water well, because I find
There's nothing plants like better than
A sprinkle with a water can.

Somehow the beans and things I grow
　　Taste better than the sort you buy.
If you could try them, you would know,
　　They're . . . different. I don't know why.
I can't explain, but there it is—
Especially the cabbages.

Rodney Bennett

Cabbages

If God were as ungenerous as man,
He would make cabbages, to feed the kine,
On some unbeautiful and heavy plan,
Meet for mere beasts. But in His craft divine
He fashions them, and colours them instead
With gold and misty blue amid the green,
Softly with purple, gallantly with red.
He curves their leaves and traces veins between;
Bejewels them with drops of rain and dew;
Caresses them with wind, and, crowning boon,
With lunar light transfigures them anew—
Great silver roses 'neath the autumn moon.

Teresa Hooley

A Perfect Lot of Lettuce

So timely sown and timely thinned,
   The soil so nicely hoed,
A sheltered place, a season kind,
   Love round them as they growed:

They hearted up by Whitsuntide,
   Though done in open ground
And Whitsun early; how my pride
   And pleasure did abound.

No blasted slugs nor wireworm came,
   Nor any frost did strike;
As clean as in a house, or frame,
   They stood there all alike.

The village housewives came with pleas,
   And offered handsome pay
To have them for the hikers' teas
   On Whitsun holiday.

I stood and hesitated long;
   To pull them seemed a shame;
For why? when only one was gone
   They would not look the same.

But there, the stuff was grown to eat,
    We should be thankful of it,
So let the hikers have their treat
    And cottage wives their profit.

They must be pulled, or run to seed.
    We will not let it fret us.
But I'll remember till I'm dead
    That perfect lot of lettuce.

Ruth Pitter

After All The Digging

and the planting
and the   pulling
of weeds
on hot summer afternoons

there are cool mornings
we can
walk between
the rows
and bite a bean   or chew a lettuce
leaf
and taste the ripe tomatoes
the
way
the rabbits
take
breakfast

Arnold Adoff

from **Seeds**

A row of pearls
Delicate green
Cased in white velvet—
The broad bean.

James Reeves

Leeks

I like the leeke above all herbes and flowers,
When first we wore the same, the field was ours.
The leeke is white and green, whereby is meant
That Britains are both stout and eminent.
Next to the lion and the unicorn
The leeke the fairest emblem that is worn.

Anon
(Ancient manuscript
British Museum)

Onions skin very thin,
Mild winter coming in;
Onions skin thick and tough,
Coming winter will be rough.

Thomas Tusser
(16th Century)

From Juan Fang The Hermit on an Autumn Day, Thirty Bundles of Winter Onions

Potherbs in the autumn garden round the house
Of my friend the hermit behind his rough-cut
Timber gate. I never wrote and asked him for them
But he's sent this basket full of Winter Onions, still
Damp with dew. Delicately grass-green bundles,
White jade small bulbs.
Chill threatens an old man's innards,
These will warm and comfort me.

Tu Fu
(written in 759 A.D.)

Fields of Asparagus

From their long narrow beds
Asparagus raise reptilian heads
(Even the sand in May awakes)
And men who think that they are snakes
With shining knives
Walk to and fro, taking their scaly lives.

My path goes to the sea
But turning round comes back to me
In clouds of wind-blown sand
Making a desert of the land,
Where men must fight
With purple snakes that grow up in a night.

Andrew Young

Picking Mushrooms

Road and milestones.
Trees and ditches.
We shuffle away
To look for mushrooms.

One by one
Dive out of daylight
To paddle
In soaking forest.

The sun, from a clearing
In thickets of darkness,
Gropes under bushes
For brown and yellow mushrooms

That lurk by a tree-stump,
A bench for a bird.
We've only our shadows
For signposts.

September rations
So brief the hours,
The twilight fumbles
And fails to find us.

Home with our baskets
Stuffed to bursting,
Pine-mushrooms
Half the haul.

Behind us the day,
Stonewalled by the forest,
Burns swiftly down
In worldly splendour.

Boris Pasternak

Parsnips

If you want a parsnip good and sweet,
Sow it in March when you sow your wheat

Thomas Tusser

Corn Must Be Sown

Fall gently and still, good corn,
   Lie warm in thy earthy bed:
And stand so yellow some morn—
   For beast and man must be fed.

Thomas Carlyle

Blow, Wind, Blow

Blow, wind, blow! and go, mill, go!
That the miller may grind his corn;
That the baker may take it,
And into bread make it,
And send us some hot in the morn.

Anon

The Windmill

Behold! a giant am I!
  Aloft here in my tower,
  With my granite jaws I devour
The maize, the wheat, and the rye,
And grind them into flour.

I look down over the farns;
  In the fields of grain I see
  The harvest that is to be,
And I fling to the air my arms,
  For I know it is all for me.

I hear the sound of flails
  Far off, from the threshing-floors
  In barns, with their open doors,
And the wind, the wind in my sails,
  Louder and louder roars.

I stand here in my place,
  With my foot on the rock below,
  And whichever way it may blow
I meet it face to face,
  As a brave man meets his foe.

And while we wrestle and strive,
  My master, the miller, stands
  And feeds me with his hands;
For he knows who makes him thrive,
  Who makes him lord of lands.

On Sundays I take my rest;
  Churchgoing bells begin
  Their low, melodious din;
I cross my arms on my breast,
  And all is peace within.

H. W. Longfellow

Sweet Chestnuts

How still the woods were! Not a redbreast whistled
To mark the end of a mild autumn day.
Under the trees the chestnut-cases lay,
Looking like small green hedgehogs softly bristled.

Plumply they lay, each with its fruit packed tight;
For when we rolled them gently with our feet,
The outer shells burst wide apart and split,
Showing the chestnuts brown and creamy-white.

Quickly we kindled a bright fire of wood,
And placed them in the ashes. There we sat,
Listening how all our chestnuts popped and spat.
And then, the smell how rich, the taste how good!

John Walsh

Two Penn'orth of Chestnuts

Two penn'orth of Chestnuts!
Two penn'orth of Chestnuts!
If they come from Spain
You may take them back again!
If they come from Italy
I'll refuse them bitterly!
But if they come from Houghton Wood
I'll know they are little and sweet and good.

Eleanor Farjeon

Bee

You want to make some honey?
All right. Here's the recipe.
Pour the juice of a thousand flowers
Through the sweet tooth of a Bee.

X. J. Kennedy

Honey is like the morning sun
It has all the grace of summer
And the mellow freshness of the fall.

Lorca

Sing a Song of Honey

Honey from the white rose, honey from the red,
Is not that a pretty thing to spread upon your bread?
When the flower is open, the bee begins to buzz,
I'm very glad, I'm very glad, I'm very glad it does—
Honey from the lily,
    Honey from the May,
AND the dafodilly,
    AND the lilac spray—
When the snow is falling, when the fires are red,
Is not that a pretty thing to spread upon your bread?

Honey from the heather, honey from the lime,
Is not that a dainty thing to eat in winter-time?
Honey from the cherry, honey from the ling,
Honey from the celandine that opens in the Spring.
Honey from the clover,
    Honey from the pear—
Summer may be over,
    But I shall never care.
When the fires are blazing, honey from the lime
Makes a very dainty dish to eat in winter-time.

Kings will leave their counting any time they're told,
Queens are in the parlour spreading honey gold,
Gold from honeysuckle, gold from lupins' spire—
Who will stay in counting-house and miss the parlour
                                                fire?

Honey from the daisy,
   Honey from the plum,
Kings will all be lazy,
   And glad that Winter's come.
Who will keep to counting till the sum is told?
I'll be in the parlour and eating honey-gold.

Barbara Euphan Todd

Apple Song

I am an apple
I swing on the tree
I have a sharpness
At the heart of me

And no sun at noonday
Brutal with heat
Can utterly tame me
And render me sweet

Don't eat me on picnics
At height of midsummer
With lettuce and radish
Tomatoes, cucumber

When your body is tanned
And your mind thick as cream
And all life a languorous
Strawberry dream

27

But when Autumn is stirred
By a spoon of a wind
And the clothes you are wearing
Seem suddenly thinned

And your walk through the orchard
Is vaguely beset
By currents of feeling—
Nostalgia, regret,

And you need an assurance
That December and June
Can be blended together,
Pluck me down. Eat me then.

Brian Jones

Apples

Behold the apples' rounded worlds:
juice-green of July rain,
the black polestar of flower, the rind
mapped with its crimson stain.

The russet, crab and cottage red
burn to the sun's hot brass,
then drop like sweat from every branch
and bubble in the grass

They lie as wanton as they fall,
and where they fall and break,
the stallion clamps his crunching jaws,
the starling stabs his beak.

In each plump gourd the cidery bite
of boys' teeth tears the skin;
the waltzing wasp consumes his share,
the bent worm enters in.

I, with as easy hunger, take
entire my season's dole;
welcome the ripe, the sweet, the sour,
the hollow and the whole.

Laurie Lee

Moonlit Apples

At the top of the house the apples are laid in rows,
And the skylight lets the moonlight in, and those
Apples are deep-sea apples of green.   There goes
  A cloud on the moon in the autumn night.

A mouse in the wainscot scratches, and scratches, and
   then
There is no sound at the top of the house of men
Or mice; and the cloud is blown, and the moon again
  Dapples the apples with deep-sea light.

They are lying in rows there, under the gloomy beams,
On the sagging floor; they gather the silver streams
Out of the moon, those moonlit apples of dreams,
  And quiet is the steep stair under.

In the corridors under there is nothing but sleep,
And stiller than ever on orchard boughs they keep
Tryst with the moon, and deep is the silence, deep
  On moon-washed apples of wonder.

John Drinkwater

from **Cider-House**

Only a few remember the cider days,
the shuffle of clogged feet on the littered floor,
fruit piled high in the round baskets,
trundled in from the warm harvesting,
the nodding horses waiting patiently by the orchard gate,
waggons bumping along the ruts to the cool house.

And then all day the golden liquid
trickling, bubble and drop, through the creaking wood,
the engine still humming the same, soft song,
pipes, hogsheads and puncheons filled to the bung,
the raw juice heady, overflowing,
mashed straw and pulp thrown to the pigs.

They are gone now, cider-house and orchards,
the billowing tides of blossoms riding the slopes,
with early bees raiding, and Severn, a silver eel,
twisting to the sea on the far-away skyline.

The magical names remain,
those old apples of cidered Gloucestershire,
Skyrmes Kernel, Dymock Red, and Forest Styre,
Black Foxwhelps and Redstreak;
such honeyed sounds,
pure English poetry in my country ears.
I say each one to myself now, lovely on my tongue,
as ripe and rounded as cider itself,
drunk with long memories from a china mug,
the fire glowing on a winter evening.

Leonard Clark

Quinces

One year
The quinces hung like lanterns
From the tree,
Their amber sweetness harvesting
A light
That glows and trembles through
The jars;
The jelly set in slithering
Rounds of glass
Hoarding the taste of autumn's
Heavy gold;
Melting the ice of winter
From our tongues.

Lotte Kramer

Fruit gathered too soon will taste of the wood,
Will shrink and be bitter, and seldom taste good:
So fruit that is shaken, and beat off a tree,
With bruising and falling, soon faulty will be.

Thomas Tusser

Q is for Quince

The Quince tree has a silken flower,
　The Quince tree has a downy fruit,
The Quince tree is a curious bower
　Of greeny leaves and gnarly root.
Its shape is like a witch grown old,
　Its flowers like fairies, and it bears
Quinces that when their down turns gold
　Look still more beautiful than pears.
And oh, whoever smells the Quince
　Knows that the fairies must have placed
The scent there—*but don't taste it, since*
　It was the Witch who made the taste!

Eleanor Farjeon

The Gooseberry Tree

Some pilgrim-folk sing of the oak for bedsteads,
The ash-tree for staves, or the thorn to thwack heads,
But I think the most wonderful tree to me
Is the foolish and frumpy-leaved gooseberry tree,

For when I eat gooseberry pudding or tart
Zig-zag goes my brain, and away whirls my heart,
I'm a schoolboy again with my wits on the roam,
And I'm having great joy in our garden at home;
It was chock-full of gooseberries dropping to waste,
Even more than you needed for stewing or paste.

And the garden was hooked to a crooked old street,
And the street crawled away to high moorlands of peat,
And the moorlands fell softly in waves to the West,
And the West concealed God and the homes of the blest;
Such a wild Pennine country of moss, fern and heath,
With the trout beck aswirl in the valley beneath.

So when I eat gooseberry pudding or tart
From the back of my forehead the rolling hills start;
My thoughts are disturbed by loud dinning streams,
And my brain sits aloft in the saddle of dreams;
I am glad, I am sad, I am merry and mad,
And the stars seem so near seen with eyes of a lad.

Forgive me my trespasses, Lord, and be nice,
Boil me gooseberry pudding in Paradise.

Herbert Palmer

Bilberries

On the hillside
in shaggy coats
hobgoblin fruit
easy for little
hands

Gerda Mayer

from **Blueberries**

'You ought to have seen what I saw on my way
To the village, through Patterson's pasture today:
Blueberries as big as the end of your thumb,
Real sky-blue, and heavy, and ready to drum
In the cavernous pail of the first one to come!
And all ripe together, not some of them green
And some of them ripe! You ought to have seen . . .

You ought to have seen how it looked in the rain,
The fruit mixed with water in layers of leaves,
Like two kinds of jewels, a vision for thieves.'

Robert Frost

*September blow soft
Till fruit be in loft.*

Thomas Tusser

Blackberries

Wind roaring loud!
Sky a black cloud,
With fear of thunder!
Weather not heeding,
I run, scratched and bleeding,
Back home with my plunder.

And though Mother's holding
My hand and scolding,
How can I listen?—
So ripe and sweet they are,
Where in their glassy jar
They blackly glisten.

John Walsh

Blackberry

Hedge is like a breaking wave;
Thorns are stinging like the sea.—
Lean tiptoe, or plunge, to pick
Sparkling clustered blackberry.

Savage little eyes they keep
Blinking through their juicy spray.
Every-hidden-where they peep,
Tantalising us all day.

Oh, a wild and dusky store,
Plentiful and free to all:
We will keep a Blackberry Feast—
Bramble-jelly-festival.

Boys with baskets empty-full,
Girls, with happy laughter, singing,
Wander everywhere to pull.
Small sweet children call and run
And prick their little fingers; autumn sun
Glitters over everyone.

Everybody will be bringing
Fragrant loads by field and hill
Homeward into Blackberry Mill.

Harold Monro

Mango, Little Mango

The mango stands for Africa
    in its taste
    in its smell
    in its colour
    in its shape

The mango has the shape of a heart—
    Africa too!
It has a taste that's hot, strong and sweet—
    Africa too!

It has a reddy-brown shade
    like the tanned plains
    of my beloved earth
Because of this I love you and your taste
    Mango!
    Heart of fruit, sweet and mild.

    You are the love of Africa
because beating in your breast
    Is Africa's heart,
    O, mango, little mango,
    love of Africa.

Anon
(Translated by Chris Searle)

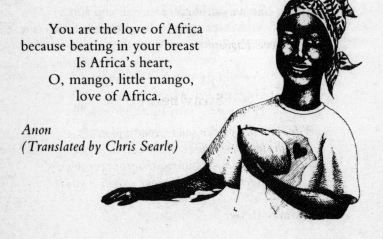

Millions of Strawberries

Marcia and I went over the curve,
Eating our way down
Jewels of strawberries we didn't deserve;
Eating our way down,
Till our hands were sticky, and our lips painted,
And over us the hot day fainted,
And we saw snakes,
And got scratched,
And a lust overcame us for the red unmatched
Small buds of berries,
Till we lay down—
Eating our way down—
And rolled in the berries like two little dogs,
Rolled in the late gold.
And gnats hummed,
And it was cold,
And home we went, home without a berry,
Painted red and brown,
Eating our way down.

Genevieve Taggard

Strawberry

Wife, into thy garden, and set me a plot
*   With strawberry roots, of the best to be got:*
Such growing abroad, among thorns in the wood,
*   Well-chosen and picked, prove excellent good.*

Thomas Tusser

Bread and Cherries

'Cherries, ripe cherries!'
   The old woman cried,
In her snowy white apron,
   And basket beside;
And the little boys came,
   Eyes shining, cheeks red,
To buy bags of cherries
   To eat with their bread.

Walter de la Mare

A Prayer

O Ceres, from whose copious horn
flows the gold corn,
the young lettuce and green
pea, the mushroom, the bean,
the sweet red cherry,
the new potato and the strawberry—
Thou, from whom life itself so bounteously comes,
please, *please*, PLEASE no more plums!

Virginia Graham

Shopping

Supermarket

I'm
lost
among a
maze of cans,
behind a pyramid
of jams, quite near
asparagus and rice,
close to the Oriental spice,
and just before sardines.
I hear my mother calling, 'Joe.
Where are you, Joe? Where did you
Go?' And I reply in a voice concealed among
the candied orange peel, and packs of Chocolate
                                 Dreams.

     'I
     hear
     you, Mother
     dear, I'm here—
     quite near the ginger ale
     and beer, and lost among a
               maze
             of cans
           behind a
         pyramid of jams
        quite near asparagus
      and rice, close to the
  Oriental spice, and just before sardines.'

But
still
my mother
calls me, 'Joe!
Where are you, Joe?
Where did you go?'
'Somewhere
around asparagus
that's in a sort of
broken glass,
beside a kind of m-
ess-
y jell
that's near a tower of cans that f
e
l
l
and squashed the Chocolate Dreams.'

Felice Holman

The Friendly Cinnamon Bun

Shining in his stickiness and glistening with honey,
Safe among his sisters and his brothers on a tray,
With raisin eyes that looked at me as I put down my
     money,
There smiled a friendly cinnamon bun, and this I heard
     him say:

'It's a lovely, lovely morning, and the world's a lovely
     place;
I know it's going to be a lovely day.
I know we're going to be good friends; I like your honest
     face;
Together we might go a long, long way.'

The baker's girl rang up the sale, 'I'll wrap your bun,'
     said she.
'Oh no, you needn't bother,' I replied.
I smiled back at that cinnamon bun and ate him, one two
     three,
And walked out with his friendliness inside.

Russell Hoban

For Strawberries

> Ripe, ripe Strawberries!
> Who'll buy Strawberries?
Buy my Strawberries red and sweet!
Then your Child can have a Treat,
And I'll trudge Home and rest my Feet,
And cry no more in the dusty Street,
> Ripe, ripe Strawberries!
> Who'll buy Strawberries?

Eleanor Farjeon

Strawberry Town

Out there in the sunny fields, they are gathering the
    strawberry-crops
Into thin white plaited baskets, each with its fruit heaped
    high;
And here in the busy street, under the striped blinds of
    the shops,
The strawberries are stacked in the open, just where they
    will catch the eye.

And inside the shops there are more of
    them—strawberries in crimson piles
Poured out among the earthy brown potatoes and green-
    shelled peas;
The housewives chatter and laugh; the shopman serves
    and smiles;
And the air is scented and rich with the thought of
    strawberry-teas.

School-children, sauntering home in the heat of the
    afternoon,
Stop short at the sight of those strawberries, and stare,
    and wonder, and dream:
They see them all pinky-and-white, sliced up with a
    silver spoon,
And powdered with fine white sugar, and thickened
    with yellow cream.

But the tame old jackdaw, perched up high on the
    garden-wall,
Has his dream too. You watch him!—Suddenly, down
    he's flown!
He's snatched up the reddest, pulpiest, juiciest
    strawberry of all—
And off to some shady corner, to feast there all on his
    own!

John Walsh

I Can't Abear

I can't abear a Butcher,
   I can't abide his meat,
The ugliest shop of all is his,
   The ugliest in the street;
Bakers' are warm, cobblers' dark,
   Chemists' burn watery lights;
But oh, the sawdust butcher's shop,
   That ugliest of sights!

Walter de la Mare

Turkeys Observed

One observes them, one expects them;
Blue-breasted in their indifferent mortuary,
Bleached bare on the cold marble slabs
In immodest underwear frills of feather.

The red sides of beef retain
Some of the smelly majesty of living:
A half-cow slung from a hook maintains
That blood and flesh are not ignored.

But a turkey cowers in death.
Pull his neck, pluck him, and look—
He is just another poor forked thing,
A skin bag plumped with inky putty.

He once complained extravagantly
In an overture of gobbles;
He lorded it on the claw-flecked mud
With a grey flick of his Confucian eye.

Now, as I pass the bleak Christmas dazzle,
I find him ranged with his cold squadrons:
The fuselage is bare, the proud wings snapped,
The tail-fin stripped down to a shameful rudder.

Seamus Heaney

Rathmines Shopping Centre

Magazine faces smile,
begging to be bought.

An orange-mouthed young girl
Flicks away her ice-pop stick.

Tomatoes, celery and lettuce
are richly displayed for the hungry:

but the poor red-brown loinchop
shows only its solitary gleaming blood-drop.

Alan Moore

Turnip-Tops

While yet the white frost sparkles over the ground,
  And daylight just peeps from the misty blue sky,
In yonder green fields with my basket I'm found;
  Come, buy my sweet turnip-tops—turnip-tops buy.

Sadly cold are my fingers, all drenched with the dew,
  For the sun has scarce risen the meadows to dry;
And my feet have got wet with a hole in my shoe;
  Come haste, then, and buy my sweet turnip-tops, buy.

While you are asleep, with your bed-curtains drawn,
  On pillows of down, in your chambers so high,
I trip with the first rosy beam of the morn,
  To cull the green tops:—come, my turnip-tops buy.

Then with the few halfpence or pence I can earn,
  A loaf for my poor mammy's breakfast I'll buy,
And tomorrow again little Ann shall return,
  With turnip-tops, green, and fresh-gathered, to cry.

Ann Taylor

Against Broccoli

The local groceries are all out of broccoli;
Loccoli.

Roy Blount

The Fishmonger

Sleek through his fingers
the fishes slide,
glisten and curve
and slap their tails
on the smooth white slab . . .

silver on marble
ranged they lie.

The fishmonger's hands
are cold with eternal
halibut, haddock,
hake and cod;

his arms are swollen
and red beside
the delicate silver
of the slender fishes;

but his eyes are glazed
and dull like theirs
and his mouth gapes
in codlike wonder

at the flickering stream
that slips through his fingers!

A. S. J. Tessimond

from **Miss Thompson Goes Shopping**

*(She visits the Fishmonger after leaving the bootshop where she
was tempted by a pair of slippers.)*

A little further down the way
Stands Miles's fish shop, whence is shed
So strong a smell of fishes dead
That people of a subtler sense
Hold their breath and hurry thence.
Miss Thompson hovers there and gazes.
Her housewife's knowing eye appraises
Salt and fresh, severley cons
Kippers bright as tarnished bronze;
Great cods disposed upon the sill,
Chilly and wet with gaping gill,
Flat head, glazed eye, and mute, uncouth,
Shapeless, wan, old-woman's mouth.
Next, a row of soles and plaice,
With querulous and twisted face,
And red-eyed bloaters, golden-grey;
Smoked haddocks ranked in neat array;
A group of smelts that take the light
Like slips of rainbow, pearly bright;
Silver trout with rosy spots,
And coral shrimps with keen black dots
For eyes, and hard and jointed sheath
And crisp tails curving underneath.
But there upon the sanded floor,
More wonderful in all that store
Than anything on slab or shelf,
Stood Miles the fishmonger himself.
Foursquare he stood and filled the place.

His huge hands and his jolly face
Were red. He had a mouth to quaff
Pint after pint: a sounding laugh,
But wheezy at the end, and oft
His eyes bulged outwards and he coughed.
Aproned he stood from chin to toe.
The apron's vertical long flow
Warped grandly outwards to display
His hale, round belly hung midway,
Whose apex was securely bound
With apron-strings wrapped round and round.
Outside Miss Thompson, small and staid,
Felt, as she always felt, afraid
Of this huge man who laughed so loud
And drew the notice of the crowd.

Awhile she paused in timid thought,
Then promptly hurried in and bought
'Two kippers, please. Yes, lovely weather.'
'Two kippers? Sixpence altogether.'
And in her basket laid the pair
Wrapped face to face in newspaper.

Then on she went, as one half blind,
For things were stirring in her mind.
Then turned about with fixed intent,
And, heading for the bootshop, went

Straight in and bought the scarlet slippers,
And popped them in beside the kippers.

Martin Armstrong

Fish and Chips

Fish and chips today for tea,
A fish for Gran, a fish for me.
I buy them at the corner place,
From smiling Meg of rosy face.

Meg sees the small boys lick their lips
At battered fish and golden chips.
Her apron's white, her hands are red;
She sees the hungry thousands fed.

For sixpence more there're peas as well,
Mushy peas with gorgeous smell;
And butter beans on Friday night,
Pale, steaming beans for your delight.

The counter's white the walls are pink,
The shelves hold lemonade to drink.
The fat is hissing in the pan,
And soon I hurry home to Gran.

The chips look good they taste the same,
They've won our Meg some local fame.
Fish and chips today for tea,
A fish for Gran, a fish for me.

A. Elliott-Cannon

Song of the Supermarket

COME IN! COME IN! COME IN!
   Sings the SUPERMARKET.
With my voice like silver coins,
   It is I who ask it.
Use trolley with squealing wheels
   Or wire basket.

Come in! I am waiting for you,
   MUZAK is playing.
And stands at the ends of aisles
   BEST BUYS displaying,
CHEAPEST AND BEST for miles,
   My clients are saying.

Is it Vegetables and Fruit?
   They are all SELECTED
From Farm and Orchard . . . Meat or Cheese?
   They're PROTECTED
BY REFRIGERATION, prepared, prepacked,
   Predigested.

Go where you like, choose what you will,
   Spend all day here.
All you need, all you wish,
   Is on display here.
But you've finished? Your list's complete?
   Then you PAY HERE!

Leslie Norris

Cooking

from **Smells**

Why is it that the poets tell
So little of the sense of smell?
These are the odours I love well:

The smell of coffee, freshly ground;
Of rich plum pudding, holly-crowned;
Or onions fried, and deeply browned.

Christopher Morley

from **Villa L'Allegria**

Teresa the Cook

Teresa, the cook, was biscuit-coloured
  As if taken straight out of her own oven:
Her kitchen, a neat nest of Mediterranean splendours,
Flashed with fresh anchovies and fresh sardines in blue
    and silver;
There were mounds of tomatoes, baskets of eggs,
And even an octopus, its tentacles still fluttering,
Hidden out of sight, unless one knew where to look,
Behind the pudding-bowls of sugared cherries and
    candied apricots,
Under the hanging bunches of dried herbs.

There she stood, firmly, with a cook's weight visible in
      her stance,
            Laughing with white teeth, but always busy,
Against the sizzle and hiss of oil in frying-pans
That supplied a perpetual music for her activities.

Osbert Sitwell

Aunt Emmeline

She's aunt to nearly half the town;
It keeps her busy making brown
And crusty doughnuts—biscuits too.
She never says how many you
May safely eat; they're on the shelf,
You simply go and help yourself!
Her kitchen's warm with baking pies,
Her pantry sweet with jam and spice,
And she herself is plump and wise
With kindliness behind her eyes
And wrinkles all about. I go
To see her every day or so.

Rachel Field

from **The Chair**

. . .But most I loved
To watch when you stirred
Busily like a bird
At household doings; with hands floured
Mixing a magic with your cakes and tarts.

John Freeman

Baking Day

Thursday was baking day in our house.
The spicy smell of new baked bread would meet
My nostrils when I came home from school and there
    would be
Fresh buns for tea, but better still were the holidays.

Then I could stay and watch the baking of the bread.
My mother would build up the fire and pull out the
    damper
Until the flames were flaring under the oven; while it was
    heating
She would get out her earthenware bowl and baking
    board.

Into the crater of flour in the bowl she would pour sugar
And yeast in hot water; to make sure the yeast was fresh
I had often been sent to fetch it from the grocer that
    morning,
And it smelt of the earth after rain as it dissolved in the
    sweet water.

Then her small stubby hands would knead and pummel
The dough until they became two clowns in baggy
    pantaloons,
And the right one, whose three fingers and blue stump
Told of the accident which followed my birth, became
    whole.

As the hands worked a creamy elastic ball
Took shape and covered by a white cloth was set
On a wooden chair by the fire slowly to rise:
To me the most mysterious rite of all.

From time to time I would peep at the living dough
To make sure it was not creeping out of the bowl.
Sometimes I imagined it possessed, filling the whole
    room,
And we helpless, unable to control its power to grow,

But as it heaved above the rim of the bowl mother
Was there, taking it and moulding it into plaited loaves
And buns and giving me a bit to make into a bread man,
With currant eyes, and I, too, was a baker.

My man was baked with the loaves and I would eat him
    for tea.
On Friday night, when the plaited loaves were placed
Under a white napkin on the dining table,
Beside two lighted candles, they became holy.

No bread will ever be so full of the sun as the pieces
We were given to eat after prayers and the cutting of this
    bread.
My mother, who thought her life had been narrow, did
    not want
Her daughters to be bakers of bread. I think she was
    wise.

Yet sometimes, when my cultivated brain chafes at
    kitchen
Tasks, I remember her, patiently kneading dough
And rolling pastry, her untutored intelligence
All bent towards nourishing her children.

Rosemary Joseph

Mother Shelling Peas

The sun shone strongly through the window
Lighting up the dancing particles of dust
Making mother's hair gleam
Like polished brass
Shining on her black shoes
On the red tiles
As she perched on the kitchen stool
Shelling peas.
Mother's hands are quick and deft
As they move from pod to pod
Throwing empty pods in one pile
And picking up a fresh one
From the brown paper bag
Like a fisherman, gutting fish.
As she splits the pod,
The green peas are revealed
Shining, like balls of green jade.
They cling to the pod
Like a child to its mother,
But unlike a child
They are parted at a touch
And patter, like green rain
On to the other peas below.

The green of the peas
Against the white of the bowl
Looks like green grass, peeping through the snow
At the beginning of a thaw
And as more peas patter down
It is as if the snow were melting, to reveal
A hill of green,
Each empty pod looks like
The green beak of some bird.
Empty, useless, soon to be thrown away
Their time of usefulness is done.
But all peas are wasted
As far as I'm concerned
Simply because . . .
I don't like peas!

Katherine Board

Dearly beloved brethren is it not a sin,
When you peel potatoes to throw away the skin?
Skin feeds pigs,
Pigs feed you;
Dearly beloved brethren is this not true?

Anon

Recipe for Salad

To make this condiment, your poet begs
The pounded yellow of two hard-boiled eggs,
Two boiled potatoes, passed through kitchen-sieve,
Smoothness and softness to the salad give;
Let onion atoms lurk within the bowl,
And, scarce suspected, animate the whole.
Of mordant mustard add a single spoon,
Distrust the condiment that bites so soon;
But deem it not, thou man of herbs, a fault,
To add a double quantity of salt.
And, lastly, o'er the flavoured compound toss
A magic soup-spoon of anchovy sauce.
Oh, green and glorious! Oh, herbaceous treat!
'Twould tempt the dying anchorite to eat;
Back to the world he'd turn his fleeting soul,
And plunge his fingers in the salad bowl!
Serenely full, the epicure would say,
Fate cannot harm me, I have dined today.

Sydney Smith
(19th Century)

To Stew a Rump-Steak

Wash it well, and season it hot,
Bind it, and put it in the pot;
Fry three onions, put them to it,
With carrots, turnips, cloves, and suet;
With broth or gravy cover up,
Put in your spoon, and take a sup;
Soft and gentle let it simmer,
Then of port put in a brimmer;
With judgement let the ketchup flow,
Of vinegar a glass bestow;
Simmer again for half an hour,
Serve at six, and then devour.

Anon

Gourds

First cut the gourds in slices, and then run
Threads through their breadth, and dry them in the air;
Then smoke them hanging them above the fire;
So that the slaves may in the winter season
Take a large dish and fill it with the slices,
And feast on them on holidays: meanwhile
Let the cook add all sorts of vegetables,
And throw them seed and all into the dish;
Let them take strings of gherkins fairly wash'd,
And mushrooms, and all sorts of herbs in bunches,
And curly cabbages, and add them too.

Nicander
(2nd Century BC)

Apple-Pie

Of all the delicates which Britons try
To please the palate or delight the eye,
Of all the sev'ral kinds of sumptuous fare,
There is none that can with applepie compare.

Ranged in thick order let your Quinces lie,
They give a charming relish to the Pie.
If you are wise you'll not brown sugar slight,
The browner (if I form my judgment right)
A deep vermilion tincture will dispense,
And make your Pippin redder than the Quince.

When this is done there will be wanting still
The just reserve of cloves and candied peel;
Nor can I blame you, if a drop you take
Of orangewater for perfuming's sake.
But here the nicety of art is such,
There must not be too little nor too much.

O be not, be not tempted, lovely Nell!
While the hot-piping odours strongly smell,
While the delicious fume creates a gust,
To lick the o'erflowing juice or bite the crust.

You'll rather stay (if my advice may rule)
Until the hot is corrected by the cool;
Till you've infused a luscious store of cream,
And changed the purple for a silver stream.

William King
(1663–1712)

Cut
Out

an ugly face   with triangle eyes
and a big   tooth   mouth   for the
                   candle   glow
then scrape the seeds
               out
               and
wash them
          and put them
in a flat and shallow
               pan
in a low oven
          for as long as you can wait
                 this dark night

when they are done baking
                 you
                  eat
          be   fore
          booing

Arnold Adoff

Sun Flowers

                they are so beautiful
in perfect
        circle
        rows
inside
        their collars of green
                leaves

        we hate to pick
            their seeds
                    out
                  for
        the oven pan

they will roast
        slowly

and
dry   to the
        taste
     of autumn
sun

Arnold Adoff

Nice Little Fish

I rolled them in turmeric, cummin and spice,
With masses of pepper to make them taste nice:
In lashings of sesamum oil I then fried 'em—
The pungency curled up my tongue when I tried 'em:
I neglected to wash, and got down to the dish,
And I swallowed that curry of nice little fish.

(Translated by
John Brough)
from *The Subhasitaratnakosa*

I'm a Shrimp! I'm a Shrimp!

I'm a shrimp! I'm a shrimp! Of diminutive size.
Inspect my antennae, and look at my eyes;
I'm a natural syphon, when dipped in a cup,
For I drain the contents to the latest drop up.
I care not for craw-fish, I heed not the prawn,
From a flavour especial my fame has been drawn;
Nor e'en to the crab or the lobster do yield,
When I'm properly cook'd and efficiently peeled.
Quick! quick! pile the coals—let your saucepan be deep,
For the weather is warm, and I'm sure not to keep;
Off, off with my head—split my shell into three—
I'm a shrimp! I'm a shrimp—to be eaten with tea.

Robert Brough

Roast Swan Song

Aforetime, by the waters wan,
This lovely body I put on:
In life I was a stately swan.

Ah me! Ah me!
Now browned and basted thoroughly.

The cook now turns me round and turns me.
The hurrying waiter next concerns me,
But oh, this fire, how fierce it burns me!

Ah me! Ah me!

Would I might glide, my plumage fluffing,
On pools to feel cool wind soughing,
Rather than burst with pepper-stuffing.

Ah me! Ah me!

Once I was whiter than the snow.
The fairest bird that earth could show;
Now I am blacker than the crow.

Ah me! Ah me!

Here I am dished upon the platter.
I cannot fly. Oh, what's the matter?
Lights flash, teeth clash—I fear the latter.

Ouch! . . . Ouch! . . .

Anon
(Bavaria, 13th century Translated from the Latin
by George F. Whicher)

Mother Eve's Pudding

If you want a good pudding, to teach you I'm willing,
Take two pennyworth of eggs, when twelve for a
    shilling,
And of the same fruit that Eve had once chosen,
Well pared and well chopped, at least half a dozen,
Six ounces of bread (let your maid eat the crust),
The crumbs must be grated as small as the dust,
Six ounces of currants from the stones you must sort,
Lest they break out your teeth, and spoil all your sport,
Six ounces of sugar won't make it too sweet,
Some salt and some nutmeg will make it complete,
Three hours let it boil, without hurry or flutter,
And then serve it up, without sugar or butter.

Anon

Pumpkin Pie Song

In the West there lived a maid,
She was a cook who knew her trade.
She baked sweet puddings and at harvest time,
She made delicious Pumpkin Pie.

CHORUS:
Pumpkin Pie, Pumpkin Pie,
She made a special Pumpkin Pie,
Pumpkin Pie, Pumpkin Pie,
You never tasted such Pumpkin Pie.

Now this young cook was in love with a man,
He was a gardener who worked the land,
He grew potatoes, beans and, O my,
Orange Pumpkins three feet high.

At the flower show he won the prize
For his Pumpkin of enormous size
He gave it to the cook to try,
So she made a very special Pumpkin Pie.

CHORUS

She used eggs and milk and sweet brown sugar,
Cinnamon, nutmeg and some ginger.
Special spices, for she would try,
To woo the gardener with Pumpkin Pie.

After one spoonful, his eyes began to glaze,
After two mouthfuls, he fell into a daze.
'My lovely cook, you're the apple of my eye,
I'd like to taste some more of your Pumpkin Pie.'

CHORUS

Now the gardener and the cook, they're happy as can be,
Living together with children three,
They'll be happy until they die,
With regular helpings of Pumpkin Pie.

Left-Handed Egg

Before you think twice,
I implore you, I beg,
There's no problem
About a left-handed egg.

Once you'd thought twice
You could think it absurd.
But it isn't,
I promise, I give you my word.

A left-handed egg,
Like a left-handed man,
When frying,
Prefers the left side of the pan.

John Pudney

Chocolate Milk

Oh God! It's great!
to have someone to fix you
chocolate milk
and to appreciate their doing it!
Even as they stir it
in the kitchen
your mouth is going crazy
for the chocolate milk!
The wonderful chocolate milk!

Ron Padgett

Don't Leave the Spoon
in the Syrup

The lid was off,
the spoon was in,
the syrup smelled deliciously;
I looked,
I watched,
I sniffed,
and then—
I licked it syrupticiously.

N. M. Bodecker

Burnt Carrots

burnt carrots
char
broken glass
crash
ketchup bottle
falls   the cupboard
overloaded

I rush between
the keys
the words spill
and pour orderly   the smell of burning
is far away

the kitchen hazy
and acrid
picking
translucent orange
long wedge segments
cutting off the burnt edges
transfer them
to another saucepan

brush against the cupboard door
as I reach for the
olive oil   salad dressing ahoy
the bottle falls

the battlefield fills
the ground black
with charred
vitamin C
glassy thick
red gelatinous
saucy gore   oh deprived hamburgers

a fragment makes my finger bleed

the men doze

in their separate rooms
dinner is
yesterday's memory
tomorrow's
hope
not today's task

this morning
I burnt the toast

Michelene Wandor

Salt

Salt for white
And salt for pure.
What's salted right
Will keep and cure.

Salt for cheap
And salt for free.
The poor may reap
Salt from the sea.

Salt for taste
And salt for wit.
Be wise. Don't waste
A pinch of it.

Robert Francis

Good cook to dress dinner, to bake and to brew
Deserves a reward, being honest and true.

Thomas Tusser

Eating
and
Drinking

Butterfingers

When father finished up his toast
he raised his plate for more
so mother buttered some and said,
'Don't drop it on the floor.'
'I'm not a little child!' he cried.
'I never drop my toast,'
then tipped it over on the mat . . .
   and mother laughed the most.

Peggy Dunstan

Toast

I never had a piece of toast,
Particularly long and wide,
But fell upon the sanded floor
And always on the buttered side.

James Payn

Breakfast Song in Time of Diet

Take, O take the cream away,
   Take away the sugar, too;
Let the morning coffee stay
   As a black and bitter brew.
I have gained since yesternight—
Shoot the calories on sight!

With the rising of the sun,
   Let my nourishment be bran;
Pass me, please, a sawdust bun
   To sustain the inner man.
I've put on a pound, almost—
Spread no butter on the toast!

Let the waffle and the egg
   Bask upon another's plate;
Do not offer me, I beg,
   Bacon which produces weight.
Still, I have to live till noon,
Maybe I could stand a prune.

Men, they say, have eaten pie
   With their breakfasts, and survived;
Not for such a wretch as I
   Was such revelry contrived.
Every day the scales I scan.
Doctors' orders. Pass the bran!

Stoddard King

Sausage

You may brag about your breakfast foods you eat at
    break of day,
Your crisp, delightful shavings and your stack of last
    year's hay,
Your toasted flakes of rye and corn that fairly swim in
    cream,
Or rave about a sawdust mash, an epicurean dream.
But none of these appeals to me, though all of them I've
    tried—
The breakfast that I liked the best was sausage mother
    fried.

Old country sausage was its name; the kind, of course,
    you know,
The little links that seemed to be almost as white as
    snow,
But turned unto a ruddy brown, while sizzling in the
    pan;
Oh, they were made both to appease and charm the inner
    man.
All these new-fangled dishes make me blush and turn
    aside,
When I think about the sausage that for breakfast mother
    fried.

There upon the kitchen table, with its cloth of turkey
    red,
Was a platter heaped with sausage and a plate of home-
    made bread,

And a cup of coffee waiting—not a puny demi-tasse
That can scarcely hold a mouthful, but a cup of greater
      class;
And I fell to eating largely, for I could not be denied—
Oh, I'm sure a king would relish the sausage mother
      fried.

Times have changed and so have breakfasts; now each
      morning when I see
A dish of shredded something or of flakes passed up to
      me,
All my thoughts go back to boyhood, to the days of long
      ago,
When the morning meal meant something more than
      vain and idle show.
And I hunger, Oh, I hunger, in a way I cannot hide,
For a plate of steaming sausage like the kind my mother
      fried.

Edgar A. Guest

from **Breakfast**

Give me a little ham and egg,
And let me be alone, I beg,
Give me tea, hot, sweet and weak,
Bring me *The Times* and do not speak.

A. P. Herbert

Dr Browning at Breakfast

'Will ye take a scrambled egg, Dr Browning, with your
      toast,
  Or p'raps the daintiest slice of ham or beef,
Or a snack of Finnan haddie (and ye'll pardon me the
      boast)
  O' dainties they Scots haddies are the chief;
There's porritch on the wagon, Dr Browning, if ye wish,
  And devilled kidneys comin' from below
And if ye'd wet your whistle—o' coky take a dish—'
  'Cocoa! Mrs Green, Cocoa!'

'Anchovies are beside ye and honey from the hive,
  And creases if ye'd like a bit o' green;
Or just look'ee at that lobster—in the pot at half past
      five;
  Or if it takes your fancy a sardine.
If furrin is your taste there's some Rooshan caviare
  Or them apricocks that Green himself did grow
La, and if ye'd wet your whistle there's coky, and to
      spare—'
  'Cocoa!! Mrs Green, Cocoa!!'

'Have a mushroom or a muffin, all a-swimming in its
    grease
  Or a slice of brawn, a relishin' o' mace;
Just make yeself at 'ome, Dr Browning, if ye please,
I would like to see ye plumper in the face.
Grilled trout and seedy cake, peach preserve and prawns
    in pot,
  Fried sassage, bacon, ox tongue, and cod's roe;
Why, and if ye'd wet your whistle there's coky pipin'
    hot—'
  'Cocoa!!! Mrs Green, Cocoa!!!'

Walter de la Mare

Porridge

I didn't like my porridge,
But my mummy made me have it.
So while she wasn't looking,
I gave it to my rabbit.

I gave it to my rabbit,
But he was eating carrots,
He didn't want it either,
So I gave it to my parrot.

But he was busy crunching,
Brown nuts on a big brown log.
He didn't want it either,
So I gave it to my dog.

My dog he had a juicy bone,
He didn't want it either,
So while no one was looking.
I threw it on the fire.

It hissed and steamed and sizzled,
As porridge will when burning.
And then I heard my mummy's feet,
Into the room returning.

She said, 'You ate that quickly,
Faster than I ever saw,
You must have really liked it.'
And she dished me out some more.

Clive Riche

Porridge

Dorothea, Dolly, Dot,
wouldn't eat her porridge
        hot.
Left it sitting on the table,
said,
'I'll eat it when I'm able.'

'Eat it now,'
her mother said.
'Or you'll go straight back
        to bed.'

'NO.'
Said one.
'YES.'
Said the other.
'Dorothea I'm your mother
simply do as you are told'—
'No,' said
Dolly, Dot.
'It's cold.'

Peggy Dunstan

Tomato Ketchup

If you do not shake the bottle
None'll come—and then a lot'll.

Anon

Egg Thoughts

Soft boiled
I do not like the way you slide,
I do not like your soft inside,
I do not like you many ways,
And I could do for many days
Without a soft-boiled egg.

Sunny-Side-Up
With their yolks and whites all runny
They are looking at me funny.

Sunny-Side-Down
Lying face-down on the plate
On their stomachs there they wait.

Poached
Poached eggs on toast, why do you shiver
With such a funny little quiver?

Scrambled
I eat as well as I am able,
But some falls underneath the table.

Hard-Boiled
With so much suffering today
Why do them any other way?

Russell Hoban

Little Bits of Soft-Boiled Egg

Little bits of soft-boiled egg
Spread along the table leg
Annoy a parent even more
Than toast and jam dropped on the floor.
(When you're bashing on the ketchup
Keep in mind where it may fetch up.)
Try to keep the food you eat
Off your clothes and off your seat,
On your plate and fork and knife.
This holds true throughout your life.

Fay Maschler

from **Shore Picnic**

. . . No gong summons us, no butler bends, no grimy
Fingers of waiter serve us messes slimy.
We stand, loll, lie; Wives two, husbands two and
Mixed children and a friend or two at hand,
And two by two we eat and drink and talk,
Manners forgot, so that we rise and walk,
Return, nibble like rabbits, gobble like turkeys . . .
The things we eat are things we never eat
In home's satiety, but the air gives a heat
To appetite;—brown thick crusts daubed with butter,
Lettuce washed in the endless watery mutter
Splashing down and down from height to height;
Eggs, cheese and festive shrimps, raspberries and
plums,
And wasps more plenteous . . .

John Freeman

Knoxville, Tennessee

I always like summer
best
you can eat fresh corn
from Daddy's garden
and okra
and greens
and cabbage
and lots of
barbecue
and buttermilk
and home-made ice-cream
at the church picnic

and listen to
gospel music
outside
at the church
homecoming
and go to the mountains with
your grandmother
and go barefooted
and be warm
all the time
not only when you go to bed
and sleep

Nikki Giovanni

Food out of Doors

Can't mutton be dull,
And potatoes be dull,
And pudding be dull,
    And slices of bread,
With four walls all round,
And a floor for the ground,
And a ceiling all sound
    And safe overhead?

And *can't* bread be sweet,
And slices of meat,
And pudding to eat,
What beautiful fare
With trees all around,
And grass on the ground,
And the sky full of sound
Of the birds in the air!

Eleanor Farjeon

Picnic

Ella, fell a
Maple tree.
Hilda, build a
Fire for me.

Teresa, squeeze a
Lemon, so.
Amanda, hand a
Plate to Flo.

Nora, pour a
Cup of tea.
Fancy, Nancy,
What a spree!

Hugh Lofting

Sipping Cider

The sweetest girl I ever saw
Sat sipping cider through the straw.
I said to her 'My dear, what for
Do you sip cider through a straw?'
She said 'My dear, why don't you know
That sipping cider's all the go.'
So cheek by cheek and jaw by jaw
We both sipped cider through a straw.
That's how I got my ma-in-law,
Through sipping cider through a straw.
And now I've got ten kids or more
through sipping cider through a straw.'

Camp Fire Song

When I sat next the Duchess at tea,
It was just as I knew it would be,
Her rumblings abdominal
Were something phenomenal—
And everyone thought it was me.

Anon

Lucy

Lucy was a truthful child,
nicely brought up,
sweet and mild
who always did as she was told
and *never* let her meals get cold.
Mother,
proud,
could take her out
and not feel any trace of doubt
until one very sorry day
while having lunch with Auntie Fay
Mother trustingly said,
'Lou.
I'm enjoying this aren't you?'

'No,' said Lucy truthfully.
'There's a dead fly
     in my tea.'

Peggy Dunstan

On Making Tea

The water bubbles
Should become happy;
Not angry.

The tea leaves
Should become excited;
But not violently so.

The pouring of the water
On the leaves
Should be a conception;
Not a confusion.

The union of tea and water
Should be allowed to dream;
But not to sleep.

Now follow some moments of rest.

The tea is then gently poured
Into simple, clean containers,
And served before smiling
And understanding friends.

R. L. Wilson

The Way of Tea

A friend from Yueh presented me
With tender leaves of Yen-Hsi tea,
For which I chose a kettle
Of ivory-mounted gold,
A mixing-bowl of snow-white earth.
With its clear bright froth and fragrance,
It was like the nectar of Immortals.
The first bowl washed the cobwebs from my mind—
The whole world seemed to sparkle.
A second cleansed my spirit
Like purifying showers of rain.
A third and I was one with the Immortals—
What need now for austerities
To purge our human sorrows?
Worldly people, by going in for wine,
Sadly deceive themselves.
For now I know the Way of Tea is real.

Chiao-Jên

A Nice Cup of Tea

I like a nice cup of tea in the morning,
For to start the day you see,
And at half-past eleven,
Well, my idea of Heaven,
Is a nice cup of tea.
I like a nice cup of tea with my dinner,
And a nice cup of tea with my tea,
And when it's time for bed,
There's a lot to be said
For a nice cup of tea . . .

A. P. Herbert

Dining Alfresco

One morning in the garden bed
The onion and the carrot said
Unto the parsley group:
'Oh, when shall we three meet again,
In thunder, lightning, hail or rain?'
'Alas!' replied, in tones of pain
The parsley, 'in the soup'.

Charles Stuart Calverley

Soup

I saw a famous man eating soup.
I say he was lifting a fat broth
Into his mouth with a spoon.
His name was in the newspapers that day
Spelled out in tall black headlines
And thousands of people were talking about him.

    When I saw him,
He sat bending his head over a plate
Putting soup in his mouth with a spoon.

Carl Sandburg

I Hate Greens

I hate greens!
'They're good for you,' my mother said,
'They'll make the hair curl on your head,
They'll make you grow up big and strong,
That's what your father says.' He's wrong!!

I hate greens.

Peas like bullets, beans like string,
Spinach—not like anything,
Sprouts as hard as bricks and mortar,
Slimy cabbage, slopped in water,

I hate greens.

Swamp them in tomato sauce,
Hide them in your second course,
Though they make you nearly sick,
Close your eyes and gulp them quick,

I hate greens.

Limp lettuce on a lukewarm plate,
Grit in watercress I hate,
Can't bear leeks with dirt inside,
Cauliflower with slugs that died,

I hate greens.

When we go on shopping trips,
Couldn't we have egg and chips?
Couldn't we have chips and beans?
Don't you know what hunger means?

I HATE GREENS!!!

David King

The Pig

The pig, if I am not mistaken,
Supplies us sausage, ham, and bacon.
Let others say his heart is big—
I call it stupid of the pig.

Ogden Nash

Any Part of Piggy

Any part of piggy
Is quite all right with me
Ham from Westphalia, ham from Parma
Ham as lean as the Dalai Lama
Ham from Virginia, ham from York,
Trotters, sausages, hot roast pork.
Crackling crisp for my teeth to grind on
Bacon with or without the rind on
Though humanitarian
I'm not a vegetarian.
I'm neither crank nor prude nor prig
And though it may sound infra dig
Any part of darling pig
Is perfectly fine with me.

Noel Coward

Vicarage Mutton

Hot on Sunday
Cold on Monday
Hashed on Tuesday
Minced on Wednesday
Curried Thursday
Broth on Friday
Cottage-pie Saturday.

Anon

What is Veal?

William asked how veal was made,
   His little sister smiled,
It grew in foreign climes, she said,
   And call'd him silly child.

Eliza, laughing at them both,
   Told, to their great surprise,
The meat cook boiled to make the broth,
   Once lived, had nose and eyes;

Nay, more, had legs, and walked about;
   William in wonder stood,
He could not make the riddle out,
   But begged his sister would.

Well, brother, I have had my laugh,
   And you shall have yours now,
Veal, when alive, was call'd a calf—
   Its mother was a cow.

Anon
(*From Juvenile Poems 1841*)

Point of View

Thanksgiving Dinner's sad and thankless
Christmas dinner's dark and blue
When you stop and try to see it
From the turkey's point of view.

Sunday dinner isn't sunny
Easter feasts are just bad luck
When you see it from the viewpoint
Of a chicken or a duck.

Oh how I once loved tuna salad
Pork and lobsters, lamb chops too
Till I stopped and looked at dinner
From the dinner's point of view.

Shel Silverstein

Talking Turkey:
the Turkey's Tale

Lord, Thou art bountiful
I want for nothing
(though space *is* at a premium)
I am fed all manna
of victuals, plus
(it is rumoured)
added protein

It seems the reason
for this great largesse
is some Festivity
in Thy son's name

A birthday?

Should this be so
I thank Thee that I'm brought
(albeit upside down)
to add my praises
to the general paean

But GOD
   whence comes this
     KNIFE?

Eric Millward

Eating Bamboo-Shoots

My new Province is a land of bamboo-groves:
Their shoots in spring fill the valleys and hills.
The mountain woodman cuts an armful of them
And brings them down to sell at the early market.
Things are cheap in proportion as they are common;
For two farthings, I buy a whole bundle.
I put the shoots in a great earthen pot
And heat them up along with boiling rice.
The purple nodules broken,—like an old brocade;
The white skin opened,—like new pearls.
Now every day I eat them recklessly;
For a long time I have not touched meat.
All the time I was living at Lo-yang
They could not give me enough to suit my taste.
Now I can have as many shoots as I please;
For each breath of the south-wind makes a new bamboo!

Translated by Arthur Waley

**Momma
Cooks**

with
a
  wok
      and i help
      to cut
            the
vegetables

chop
     broccoli
           for
       delicious

chinese
  dishes

I Am Learning

to move my chop
sticks
           through
the
vegetables   and
              meat
and
    through
the
   oriental
          treat

we
have
tonight
but   in
between
        my
        smiles
        and
          bites
i
write
a
message
            in
            the
sweet
        and
sour
pork

i
need
a
fork

Arnold Adoff

from **The Chef Has Imagination**
or
It's Too Hard to Do It Easy

Hark to a lettuce lover.
I consider lettuce a blessing.
And what do I want on my lettuce?
Simply a simple dressing.

But in dining-car and hostel
I grow apoplectic and dropsical;
Is this *dressing* upon my lettuce,
Or is it a melting popsicle?

A dressing is not the meal, dears,
It requires nor cream nor egg,
Nor butter nor maple sugar,
And neither the nut nor the meg.

A dressing is not a compote,
A dressing is not a custard;
It consists of pepper and salt,
Vinegar, oil, and mustard.

It is not paprika and pickles,
Let us leave those to the Teutons;
It is not a pinkish puddle
Of grenadine and Fig Newtons.

Must I journey to France for dressing?
It isn't a baffling problem;
Just omit the molasses and yoghurt,
The wheat germ, and the Pablum.

It's oil and vinegar, dears,
No need to tiddle and toil;
Just salt and pepper and mustard,
And vinegar, and oil.

Ogden Nash

Spaghetti

A plate heaped high
with spaghetti
all covered with tomato sauce
is just about my favourite meal.
It looks just like
a gigantic heap of:
steaming
            tangled
        mixed
                up
twizzled
            twisted
wound
        up
            woozled
WORMS!

I like picking them up
one at a time;
swallowing them slowly
head first,
until the tail flips
across my cheek
before finally wriggling
down my throat.
But best of all,
when I've finished eating
I go and look in a mirror
because the tomato sauce
smeared around my mouth
makes me look like a clown

Frank Flynn

The Health-Food Diner

No sprouted wheat and soya shoots
And Brussels in a cake,
Carrot straw and spinach raw,
(Today, I need a steak).

Not thick brown rice and rice pilau
Or mushrooms creamed on toast,
Turnips mashed and parsnips hashed,
(I'm dreaming of a roast).

Health-food folks around the world
Are thinned by anxious zeal,
They look for help in seafood kelp
(I count on breaded veal).

No Smoking signs, raw mustard greens,
Zucchini by the ton,
Uncooked kale and bodies frail
Are sure to make me run

Loins of pork and chicken thighs
And standing rib, so prime,
Pork chops brown and fresh ground round
(I crave them all the time).

Irish stews and boiled corned beef
and hot dogs by the scores,
or any place that saves a space
For smoking carnivores.

Maya Angelou

Dinner Tonight

                    is hiding
in a mystery of steam
from
    the bowl of
spaghetti
            and meat sauce
            and
we
    must make our way through
    oregano fogs
                    and the deadly smog
            of a grated   cheese
                                breeze
        into a parmesan dream

past
    snapping beans and over broccoli logs
    we are in pizza country
        and there is danger
                            of
                                pepperoni
                                poisoning
        until dessert

Arnold Adoff

The Custard

For second course, last night, a Custard came
To the board, so hot, as none could touch the same:
Furze, three or foure times with his cheeks did blow
Upon the Custard, and thus cooled so:
It seem'd by this time to admit the touch;
But none could eate it, 'cause it stunk so much.

Robert Herrick

Sunday Special

'Come along, troops!'

The white glazed basin lifts—

A light golden mound
Of thick suet pastry
Collapses upon itself,

And from the rough clefts
That open in its sides
A sweet steam rises;

The syrup lava, browned
Apple slices, slips down,
And round the base

Of this home-made
Hill-fort, the dip
Of the plate, the spiced juices,

Cinnamon, nutmeg, clove,

Flow, surrounding their
Once great stronghold—
A stronghold crumbling now,

Besieged

And soon to be laid waste,
Levelled off, and lost almost,
Among the routine toast

And marmalade of days.

Tom Durham

Rhubarb Pie
or
The Rival Pastrycooks

Kids are funny! you never know
How to take them. I had to go
Up to London the other day,
So I asked my neighbour across the way
To give them all their dinner, see?
She's always very kind to me.
So she agreed like, quite content;
I packed my bag and off I went.
And when I got back, pretty late,
I said to my twin girls, what's eight,
'Now Dawn and Eve', I said, 'come on,
And tell me all you been and done.
I hope that you were very good,
And nicely-mannered with your food,
And that young Charl and little Dave
And Peter didn't misbehave.
I'm certain sure that Mrs Price
Took pains to cook you something nice;
Not like your own mum, but she'd try.'
They said, 'Chop toad and roobub pie'.
'What, roobub pie, what you can't eat?
I'll have to pop across the street
And tell her that you can't abide
Puddns and pies with that inside.
Oh dear, she would be vexed, I know,
To see you go and leave it so.'

'But Mum', they said, 'we ate the lot!
It was so nice, and fresh, and hot!
We said to Mrs Price, O my,
This is a lovely Roobub Pie!'

Well, well, I thought, this is a change!
On Sunday, when I light the range,
To do the roast, and Monday's stew,
I'll make a Roobub Pie or two.

D'you think they'd touch it? Oh dear no!
They sat the whole five in a row;
They sat and looked me in the eye.
They said, "We don't like Roobub Pie'!!!
And goodness knows the reason why!

Ruth Pitter

Pudding Time

Pudding-time comes once a day;
When the meat is cleared away.
We all turn round to look to see
What the pudding's going to be.
We clap our hands if up there comes
A lovely pudding stuffed with plums;
But wholesome things, like milky rice
We do not think so very nice.

Anon

Rice Pudding

What is the matter with Mary Jane?
She's crying with all her might and main,
And she won't eat her dinner—rice pudding again—
What *is* the matter with Mary Jane?

What is the matter with Mary Jane?
I've promised her dolls and a daisy-chain,
And a book about animals—all in vain—
What *is* the matter with Mary Jane?

What is the matter with Mary Jane?
She's perfectly well, and she hasn't a pain;
But, look at her, now she's beginning again!
What *is* the matter with Mary Jane?

What is the matter with Mary Jane?
I've promised her sweets and a ride in the train,
And I've begged her to stop for a bit and explain—
What *is* the matter with Mary Jane?

What is the matter with Mary Jane?
She's perfectly well and she hasn't a pain,
And it's lovely rice pudding for dinner again!—
What *is* the matter with Mary Jane?

A. A. Milne

Cheese

A cantle of Essex cheese
Was well a foot thick
Full of maggots quick:
It was huge and great
And mighty strong meat
For the devil to eat.
It was tart and punicate.

John Skelton

Say Cheese

At Christmas the STILTON
Was spilt on the Wilton,
The rare CAMEMBERT
Was as fine as can be.
But at New Year the GRUYERE
It just went straight through yer,
The CHEDDAR was bedder
But as for the BRIE,

Aaaaaaaagh! And the PORT SALUD!
Swallow one morsel, you
Kept to your bed
For a week and a day,
And if you tried WENSLEYDALE
You quite *immensely*'d ail,
Hospital–bound
Till they wheeled you away!

No better was EMMENTHAL,
Sour and inclement, all
Cratered and pocked
Like a view of the moon!
And while some are crazy
For creamed BEL PAESE,
Myself, I'd eat forcemeat
Or horsemeat as soon!

The LEICESTER was best o'
The bunch, but the rest o'
Them curled up your stomach.
Though GLOUCESTER (times two)
And jaundiced old CHESHIRE
I'd taste under pressure,
Nothing would get me,
No, nothing would get me,
But nothing would get me
To try DANISH BLUE!

Kit Wright

The Drunkard and the Pig

It was early last December,
As near as I remember,
I was walking down the street in tipsy pride;
No one was I disturbing
As I lay down by the curbing,
And a pig came up and lay down by my side.

As I lay there in the gutter
Thinking thoughts I shall not utter,
A lady passing by was heard to say:
'You can tell a man who boozes by the company he
        chooses',
And the pig got up and slowly walked away.

Anon

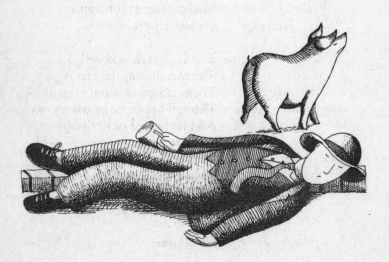

from **Ballade of Soporific Absorption**

Ho! Ho! Yes! Yes! It's very all well,
    You may drunk I am think, but I tell you I'm not,
I'm as sound as a fiddle and fit as a bell,
    And stable quite ill to see what's what.
    I under *do* stand you surprise a got
When I headed my smear with gooseberry jam:
    And I've swallowed, I grant, a beer of lot—
But I'm not so think as you drunk I am.

J. C. Squire

What I Want is a Proper
Cup O' Coffee

What I want is a proper cup of coffee
Made in a proper copper coffee pot.
I may be off my dot,
But I want a cup o' coffee
From a proper coffee pot.
Tin coffee pots and iron coffee pots,
They're no use to me;
If I can't have a proper cup o' coffee
From a proper copper coffee pot,
I'll have a cup o' tea!

R. P. Weston and Bert Lee

Coffee With the Meal

A gentlemanly gentleman, as mild as May,
Entered a restaurant famed and gay.
A waiter sat him in a draughty seat
And laughingly inquired what he'd like to eat.
'Oh I don't want venison, I don't want veal,
But I do insist on coffee with the meal.
Bring me clams in a chilly group,
And a large tureen of vegetable soup,
Steak as tender as a maiden's dream,
With lots of potatoes hashed in cream,
And a lettuce and tomato salad, please,
And crackers and a bit of Roquefort cheese,
But, waiter, the gist of my appeal,
Is coffee with, coffee with, coffee with the meal.'
The waiter groaned and he wrung his hands;
'Perhaps da headwaiter onderstands.'
Said the sleek headwaiter, like a snobbish seal,
'What, monsieur? Coffee with the meal?'
His lips drew up in scornful laughter;
'Monsieur desires a demi-tasse after!'
The gentleman's eyes grew hard as steel,
He said: 'I'm ordering coffee with the meal.
Hot black coffee in a great big cup,
Fuming, steaming, filled right up.
I don't want coffee iced in a glass,
And I don't want a miserable demi-tasse,
But what I'll have, come woe, come weal,
Is coffee with, coffee with, coffee with the meal.'
The headwaiter bowed like a poppy in the breeze;
'Monsieur desires coffee with the salad or the cheese?'
Monsieur said: 'Now you're getting warmer;

Coffee with the latter, coffee with the former;
Coffee with the steak, coffee with the soup,
Coffee with clams in a chilly group;
Yes, and with a cocktail I could do,
So bring me coffee with the cocktail, too.
I'll fight to the death for my bright ideal,
Which is coffee with, coffee with, coffee with the meal.'
The headwaiter swivelled on a graceful heel;
'Certainly, certainly, coffee with the meal!'
The waiter gave an obsequious squeal,
'Yes sir, yes sir, coffee with the meal!'
Oh what a glow did Monsieur feel
At the warming vision of coffee with the meal.
One hour later Monsieur, alas!
Got his coffee in a demi-tasse.★

Ogden Nash

★ *a demi-tasse is a small, or ½ sized coffee cup.*

Epitaph

Here lies, cut down like unripe fruit,
The wife of Deacon Amos Shute.
She died of drinking too much coffee,
Anny, Dominy, eighteen forty.

Anon

If We Didn't Have to Eat

Life would be an easy matter
  If we didn't have to eat.
    If we never had to utter,
      'Won't you pass the bread and butter,
Likewise push along that platter
  Full of meat?'
    Yes, if food were obsolete
    Life would be a jolly treat,
If we didn't—shine or shower,
Old or young, 'bout every hour—
    Have to eat, eat, eat, eat, eat—
      'Twould be jolly if we didn't have to eat.

We could save a lot of money
  If we didn't have to eat.
    Could we cease our busy buying,
    Baking, broiling, brewing, frying,
Life would then be oh, so sunny
  And complete;
  And we wouldn't fear to greet
  Every grocer in the street
If we didn't—man and woman,
Every hungry, helpless human—
  Have to eat, eat, eat, eat, eat—
  We'd save money if we didn't have to eat.

All our worry would be over
  If we didn't have to eat.
    Would the butcher, baker, grocer
    Get our hard-earned dollars? No, Sir!
We would then be right in clover
  Cool and sweet.
  Want and hunger we could cheat,
  And we'd get there with both feet,
If we didn't—poor or wealthy,
Halt or nimble, sick or healthy—
  Have to eat, eat, eat, eat, eat,
  We could get there if we didn't have to eat.

Nixon Waterman

A North Country Grace Before Meat

God Bless us All, and make us able
To eat all t'stuff what's on this table.

Snacks

Stop Thief

Come, guard this night the Christmas-pie,
That the thief, though ne'er so sly,
With his flesh-hooks, don't come nigh
      To catch it

From him who all alone sits there,
Having his eyes still in his ear,
And a deal of nightly fear,
      To watch it.

Robert Herrick

Nursery Rhyme for the
Tender-Hearted

Scuttle, scuttle, little roach—
How you run when I approach:
Up above the pantry shelf,
Hastening to secrete yourself.

Most adventurous of vermin,
How I wish I could determine
How you spend your hours of ease,
Perhaps reclining on the cheese.

Cook has gone, and all is dark—
Then the kitchen is your park:
In the garbage heap that she leaves
Do you browse among the tea leaves?

132

How delightful to suspect
All the places you have trekked:
Does your long antenna whisk its
Gentle tip across the biscuits?

Do you linger, little soul,
Drowsing in our sugar bowl?
Or, abandonment most utter,
Shake a shimmy on the butter?

Do you chant your simple tunes
Swimming in the baby's prunes?
Then, when dawn comes, do you slink
Homeward to the kitchen sink?

Timid roach, why be so shy?
We are brothers, thou and I.
In the midnight, like yourself,
I explore the pantry shelf!

Christopher Morley

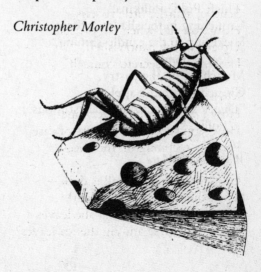

A—Apple Pie

Little Pollie Pillikins
Peeped into the kitchen,
'H'm,' says she, 'Ho,' says she,
  'Nobody there!'
Only little meeny mice,
Miniken and miching
On the big broad flagstones, empty and bare.

Greedy Pollie Pillikins
Crept into the pantry,
There stood an Apple Pasty,
  Sugar white as snow.
Off the shelf she toppled it,
Quick and quiet and canty,
And the meeny mice they watched her
  On her tip-tap-toe.

'Thief, Pollie Pillikins!'
Crouching in the shadows there,
Flickering in the candle-shining,
  Fee, fo, fum!
Munching up the pastry,
Crunching up the apples,
'Thief!' squeaked the smallest mouse,
  'Pollie, spare a crumb!'

Walter de la Mare

The Apple Song

Tap me with your finger,
rub me with your sleeve,
hold me, sniff me, peel me
curling round and round
till I burst out white and cold
from my tight red coat
and tingle in your palm
as if I'd melt and breathe
a living pomander
waiting for the minute
of joy when you lift me
to your mouth and crush me
and in taste and fragrance
I race through your head
in my dizzy dissolve.

I sit in the bowl
in my cool corner
and watch you as you pass
smoothing your apron.
Are you thirsty yet?
My eyes are shining.

Edwin Morgan

A Bowl of Fruit

In the wooden bowl
(wood coloured) are 4 apples,
3 pears and an orange.
Can you see them?

What colour are the pears?
Green? Correct. (Although
they might have been yellow.)

The apples? Wrong.
3 green and one red.

The orange? Of course,
orange. Secure in the sense
of its own glowing identity
the Lord of the Bowl
reigns over the room.
Cezanne of citrus.
Plump Picasso of peel.

Roger McGough

Peach

I lick the warm skin
  Of the ripe peach, bite gold flesh;
    juice runs down my chin.

Ian Serraillier

Melon

Summer's loud laugh
Of scarlet ice
A melon
Slice

José Juan Tablada

Watermelons

Green Buddhas
On the fruit stand.
We eat the smile
And spit out the teeth

Charles Simic

Ronde de la Grenade

A little sour is the juice of the pomegranate
    like the juice of unripe raspberries.
Waxlike is the flower
Coloured as the fruit is coloured.

Close-guarded this item of treasure, beehive partitioned,
Richness of savour,
Architecture of pentagons—
The rind splits; out tumble the seeds,
In cups of azure some seeds are blood;
On plates of enamelled bronze, others are drops of gold.

André Gide

    Write me down
As one who loved poetry
    And persimmons.

Shiki

The Lychee

Fruit white and lustrous as a pearl . . .
Lambent as the jewel of Ho, more strange
Than the saffron-stone of Hsia.
Now sigh we at the beauty of its show,
Now triumph in its taste.
Sweet juices lie in the mouth,
Soft scents invade the mind.
All flavours here are joined, yet none is master;
A hundred diverse tastes
Blend in such harmony no man can say
That one outstrips the rest. Sovereign of sweets,
Peerless, pre-eminent fruit, who dwellest apart
In noble solitude!

Wang I
(Translated from the Chinese by Arthur Waley)

Mango

Have a mango
sweet rainwashed sunripe
mango
that the birds themselves
woulda pick
if only they had seen it
a rosy miracle

Here
take it from mih hand

Star-Apple

Deepest purple
or pale green white
the star-apple is a sweet fruit
with a sweet star brimming centre
and a turn back skin
that always left me sweetly
sticky mouth

Guenips

Guenips
hanging in abundant
bunches on the fat knuckled
guenip tree
Guenips
melting like small moons
on my tongue
the succulent green gold
of the fruit kingdom

Grace Nichols

Fruit

The Nectarine on yonder wall
   Grows red, when ripened fully;
The ruddy Peach admired by all,
   Is somewhat rough and woolly.
The Apricot of amber hue,
   In tarts the taste delighting;
And purple Plum, so fair to view,
   Are equally inviting.

Anon

To a Poor Old Woman

Munching a plum on
the street a paper bag
of them in her hand

They taste good to her
They taste good
to her. They taste
good to her

You can see it by
the way she gives herself
to the one half
sucked out in her hand

Comforted
a solace of ripe plums
Seeming to feel the air
They taste good to her

William Carlos Williams

Three Plum Buns

Three plum buns
    To eat here at the stile
In the clover meadow,
    For we have walked a mile.

One for you, and one for me,
    And one left over:
Give it to the boy who shouts
    To scare sheep from the clover.

Christina Rossetti

Ice-Cream

Ice-Cream!
Is anything more delectable
Than ice-cream,
Why even the most respectable
Eat ice-cream,
It's wonderful on a summer's afternoon in June.
Ice-cream,
The recipe's something serious
But ice-cream
Makes everyone so delirious
That ice-cream
Is certainly worth the trouble that it takes . . .

Eight Scoops

'Be sure you get eight scoops,'
my Aunt Maggie tells me

but I can't see behind
the counter where the druggist
is scooping up the ice-cream
into the china bowl

so I won't really know
till I bring the bowl back
and Aunt Maggie starts
to fill the four dishes

two for Uncle Jim
two for Aunt Lizzie
two for Aunt Maggie
and two for me
unless that druggist
lost his count or secretly
hates all boys like me

Raymond Souster

you scream
I scream
everybody loves
ice-cream

Toffee-Slab

As thick as a plank, as unbending as Fate,
It was wrapped in wax-paper, and weighed like a slate;
It had a brown cow on it, smiling and fat,
With 'rich' and 'creamy' and grand words like that:

And you broke it with bricks on Mrs Doig's wall,
So it came out irregular, but with something for all
(If you were quick, it was more or less fair—
Even Wee Andy had his proportional share);

Then with nobody speaking, with sort of fixed grins
And oozings like glue leaking over our chins
We'd stand there for ages, our eyes staring wide,
The great splinters of it jammed tightly inside,

With the sharpest end stuck, up near your brain,
What pleasure!—mingled with twinges of pain.

Brian Lee

Sugarcane

When I take
a piece of sugarcane
and put it to me mouth
I does suck and suck
till all the juice come out.

I don't care
if is sun or rain
I does suck and suck
till all the juice come out.

But when I doing homewuk
and same time playing bout
Granny does tell me,
'How you can work properly
and play at the same time?
You brain can't settle.
I always telling you
you can't suck cane and whistle,
you can't suck cane and whistle!'

John Agard

Chocolate and Milk

Little Lili, whose age isn't three years quite,
Went one day with Mamma for a long country walk,
Keeping up, all the time, such a chatter and talk
Of the trees, and the flowers, and the cows, brown and
    white.
Soon she asked for some cake, and some chocolate too,
For this was her favourite lunch every day—
'Dear child,' said Mamma, 'let me see—I dare say

'If I ask that nice milkmaid, and say it's for you,
Some sweet milk we can get from her pretty white cow.'
'I would rather have chocolate,' Lili averred.
Then Mamma said, 'Dear Lili, please don't be absurd;
My darling, you cannot have chocolate now:
You know we can't get it so far from the town.—
Come and stroke the white cow,—see, her coat's soft as
    silk.'
'But, Mamma,' Lili said, 'if the *White* cow gives milk,
The chocolate surely must come from the *Brown*.'

Anon

146

Giving Potatoes

STRONG MAN: Mashed potatoes cannot hurt you, darling
Mashed potatoes mean no harm
I have brought you mashed potatoes
From my mashed potato farm.

LADY: Take away your mashed potatoes
Leave them in the desert to dry
Take away your mashed potatoes—
You look like shepherd's pie.

BRASH MAN: A packet of chips, a packet of chips,
Wrapped in the *Daily Mail*,
Golden juicy and fried for a week
In the blubber of the Great White Whale.

LADY: Take away your fried potatoes
Use them to clean your ears
You can eat your fried potatoes
With birds-eye frozen tears.

OLD MAN: I have borne this baked potato
O'er the Generation Gap,
Pray accept this baked potato
Let me lay it in your heated lap.

LADY: Take away your baked potato
In your fusty musty van
Take away your baked potato
You potato-skinned old man.

FRENCHMAN: She rejected all potatoes
For a thousand nights and days
Till a Frenchman wooed and won her
With pommes de terre Lyonnaise.

LADY: Oh my corrugated lover
So creamy and so brown
Let us fly across to Lyons
And lay our tubers down.

Adrian Mitchell

And God Said to the Little Boy

And God said to the little boy
As the little boy came out of chapel
Little boy, little boy, little boy
Did you eat that there apple?
And the little boy answered No, Lord.

And God said to the little girl
As the little girl came out of chapel
Little girl, little girl, little girl,
Did you eat that there apple?
And the little girl answered No, Lord.

Then the Lord pointed with his finger
And fixed them both with his stare,
And he said in a voice like a Rolls Royce
Well, what are them two cores doing there?

George Barker

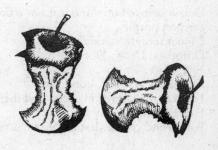

INDEX OF FIRST LINES

A cantle of Essex cheese   122
A friend from Yueh presented me   97
A gentlemanly gentleman, as mild as May   126
A little further down the way   52
A little sour is the juice of the pomegranate   138
A plate heaped high   112
A row of pearls   17
Aforetime, by the waters wan   71
After all the digging and the planting   16
Any part of piggy   103
And God said to the little boy   141
As thick as a plank, as unbending as Fate   144
At Christmas the Stilton   122
At the top of the house the apples are laid in rows   30
Before you think twice   74
Behold! a giant am I   22
Behold the apples' rounded worlds   29
Be sure you get eight scoops   143
Blow wind, blow! and go, mill go!   21
burnt carrots   76
. . .But most I loved   60
Can't mutton be dull   92
'Cherries, ripe cherries!'   40
'Come along, troops!'   116
Come, guard this night the Christmas-pie   132
Come in! Come in! Come in!   56
Cut   68
Dearly beloved brethren is it not a sin   64
Deepest purple   140
Dinner tonight is hiding   115
Dorothea, Dolly, Dot   88
Ella, fell a   93
Fall gently and still, good corn   21
First cut the gourds in slices, and then run   66
Fish and chips today for tea   55
For second course, last night, a Custard came   116

From early morning the cultivator   11
From their long narrow beds   19
Fruit gathered too soon will taste of the wood   32
Fruit white and lustrous as a pearl   139
Give me a little ham and egg   84
God Bless us All, and make us able   130
Good cook to dress dinner, to bake and brew   78
Green Buddhas   137
Guenips   140
Hark to a lettuce lover   110
Have a mango   140
Hedge is like a breaking wave   37
Here lies, cut down like unripe fruit   128
Ho! Ho! Yes! Yes! It's very all well   125
Honey from the white rose, honey from the red   26
Honey is like the morning sun   25
Hot on Sunday   103
How still the woods were! Not a redbreast whistled   24
I always like Summer   92
I am an apple   27
I can't abear a Butcher   47
I didn't like my porridge   86
I hate greens!   100
I lick the warm skin   137
I like a nice cup of tea in the morning   98
I like the leeke above all herbes and flowers   17
I never had a piece of toast   80
I rolled them in turmeric, cummin and spice   70
I saw a famous man eating soup   100
Ice-cream   142
If God were as ungenerous as man   13
If you do not shake the bottle   88
If you want a good pudding, to teach you I'm willing   72
If you want a parsnip good and sweet   21
I'm   42
I'm a shrimp! I'm a shrimp! Of diminutive size   70
In a wooden bowl   136
In the west there lived a maid   72

151

It was early last December   124
I've a garden of my own   11
Kids are funny! you never know   118
Life would be an easy matter   128
Little bits of soft-boiled egg   90
Little Lili, whose age isn't three years quite   146
Little Pollie Pillikins   134
Lord, Thou art bountiful   106
Lucy was a truthful child   95
Magazine faces smile   48
Marcia and I went over the curve   39
Mashed potatoes cannot hurt you, darling   147
Momma   108
Munching a plum on   141
My new Province is a land of bamboo-groves   107
No gong summons us, no butler bends, no grimy   91
No sprouted wheat and soya shoots   114
O Ceres, from whose copious horn   40
Of all the delicates which Britons try   67
Oh God! It's great!   75
On the Hillside   35
One morning in the garden bed   99
One observes them, one expects them   47
One year   32
Onions skin very thin   17
Only a few remember the cider days   31
Out there in the sunny fields, they are gathering the
    strawberry-crops   45
Potherbs in the autumn garden round the house   18
Pudding-time comes once a day   120
Ripe, ripe Strawberries!   45
Road and milestones   19
Salt for white   78
Scuttle, scuttle, little roach   132
September blow soft   35
She's aunt to nearly half the town   60
Shining in his stickiness and glistening with honey   44
Sleek through his fingers   50

Soft boiled   89
Some pilgrim-folk sing of the oak for bedsteads   34
So timely sown and timely thinned   14
Summer's loud laugh   137
Take, O take the cream away   81
Tap me with your finger   135
Teresa, the cook, was biscuit-coloured   58
Thanksgiving Dinner's sad and thankless   105
The lid was off   75
The local groceries are all out of broccoli   49
The mango stands for Africa   38
The Nectarine on yonder wall   141
The pig, if I am not mistaken   102
The Quince tree has a silken flower   33
The sun shone strongly through the window   63
The sweetest girl I ever saw   94
The water bubbles   96
they are so beautiful   69
Three plum buns   142
Thursday was baking day in our house   61
Today I think   10
To make this condiment, your poet begs   65
Two penn'orth of Chestnuts   24
Wash it well, and season it hot   66
What is the matter with Mary Jane?   121
What I want is a proper cup of coffee   125
When father finished up his toast   80
When I sat next the Duchess at tea   94
When I take   145
While yet the white frost sparkles over the ground   49
Why is it that the poets tell   58
Wife, into thy garden, and set me a plot   39
William asked how veal was made   104
Will ye take a scrambled egg, Dr Browning,
       with your toast   84
Wind roaring loud!   36
Write me down   138
You ought to have seen what I saw on my way   35

153

You may brag about your breakfast foods you eat
    at break of day   82
You scream   143
You want to make some honey?   25

ACKNOWLEDGEMENTS

The author and the Publisher would like to thank the
following for their kind permission to reprint
copyright material in this book:

Lothrop, Lee and Shepard Books (A Division of William
Morrow and Co Inc) and Curtis Brown Ltd for 'After
All The Digging', 'Cut out', 'Dinner Tonight', 'Momma
Cooks', and 'Sun Flowers' from *Eats* by Arnold Adoff;
The Bodley Head for 'Sugarcane' by John Agard; The
Virago Press for 'The Health-Food Diner' by Maya
Angelou from *And Still I Rise*; Martin Secker and
Warburg for 'Miss Thompson Goes Shopping' by Martin
Armstrong from *Collected Poems by Martin Armstrong*;
Faber and Faber Ltd for 'And God Said To the Little
Boy' from *To Aylsham Fair* by George Barker; The
Atlantic Monthly Co for 'Against Broccoli' by Roy
Blount Jr; The Tenth Daily Mirror Children's Literary
Competition for 'Mother Shelling Peas' by Katherine
Board; Faber and Faber Ltd for 'Don't Leave the Spoon
in the Syrup' by N M Bodecker from *Snowman Sniffles
and other verses*; Penguin Books Ltd for extract from
Poems From The Sanskrit translated by John Brough, ©
John Brough, 1968; The Estate of Leonard Clark for 'The
Cider-House' by Leonard Clark; Methuen London for
'Any Part of Piggy' by Noel Coward from *Collected
Verse*; The Literary Trustees of Walter de la Mare and
The Society of Authors as their representative for 'Bread
and Cherries', 'I Can't Abear', 'A-Apple Pie' and 'Dr
Browning at Breakfast' by Walter de la Mare; Hodder &
Stoughton Ltd for 'Porridge', 'Butterfingers', and 'Lucy'
by Peggy Dunstan; Tom Durham for 'Sunday Special'; A
Elliot-Cannon for 'Fish and Chips'; David Higham

157